AMERICAN HISTORY BY DECADE

The

1900s

Titles in the American History by Decade series are:

The 1900s
The 1910s
The 1920s
The 1930s
The 1940s
The 1950s
The 1960s
The 1970s
The 1980s
The 1990s

AMERICAN HISTORY BY DECADE

The
1900s

Deanne Durrett

KIDHAVEN
PRESS™

THOMSON

GALE

San Diego • Detroit • New York • San Francisco • Cleveland
New Haven, Conn. • Waterville, Maine • London • Munich

For more information, contact
KidHaven Press
27500 Drake Rd.
Farmington Hills, MI 48331-3535
Or you can visit our Internet site at http://www.gale.com

LIBRARY OF CONGRESS CATALOGING-IN-PUBLICATION DATA

Durrett, Deanne, 1940-
  1900s / by Deanne Durrett.
    v. cm. — (American history by decade)
  Includes bibliographical references (p.) and index.
  Contents: The Roosevelt era—Theater—The American worker—The automobile age—Glossary.
    ISBN 0-7377-1546-4 (alk. paper)
  1. United States—History—1901–1909—Juvenile literature. 2. Nineteen hundreds (Decade)—Juvenile literature. [1. United States—History—1901–1909. 2. Nineteen hundreds (Decade)] I. Title: Nineteen hundreds. II. Title. III. Series.
  E756.D87 2004
  973.91'1--dc21
                                                                              2003003555

Contents

Introduction 6
  A New Century

Chapter One 9
  The Roosevelt Era

Chapter Two 18
  Variety Theater

Chapter Three 26
  The American Worker

Chapter Four 36
  The Automobile Age

Notes 42

Glossary 43

For Further Exploration 44

Index 45

Picture Credits 47

About the Author 48

A New Century

L ife in the United States may have changed more in the first decade of the 1900s than in any other time in American history. As America entered the twentieth century and the modern age, conveniences such as telephones, electricity, and automobiles became available to many people. Ice cream cones, crayons, Jell-O, neon lights, and teddy bears came on the scene.

More products meant more factories and a need for more workers. Job opportunities lured people from the farm to the city. And the workers and their families began building America's major cities that we know today. Things looked good in America, and many immigrants came seeking jobs and the opportunity for a better life.

America was at peace in the first decade of the 1900s. For many Americans, life was good and getting better. Most people worked long hours and had few luxuries compared to today. Still, they had more than in the past, and life was simple. The 1900s decade is part of the time people remember as "the good old days."

There were many problems, however. As the nation progressed into the modern age, many people lived in poverty. In fact, most factory workers lived in poverty.

Construction workers build a skyscraper in New York in 1908.
Jobs were plentiful during the first decade of the 1900s.

Then and Now

	1900	2000
U.S. population:	75,994,575	281,421,906
Life expectancy:	White female: 47.3 White male: 46.3	Female: 79.5 Male: 74.1
Average wage of workers:	$12.98 a week (for 59 hours)	$687.94 a week (for 40 hours)
Unemployment rate:	5%	5%

Source: Kingwood College Library; National Vital Statistics Reports, Vol. 51, No. 3; U.S. Census Bureau.

They were not paid a fair wage because there were no laws to protect them. Most companies and businesspeople **exploited** the American worker and damaged the environment. Some people, political activists of the time, noticed these problems and wanted to do something about them. Theodore Roosevelt would lead them in attacking many of these problems.

CHAPTER ONE

The Roosevelt Era

The 1900s are remembered as the Roosevelt Era. President Theodore Roosevelt made many important decisions during these changing times. More than one hundred years later, America still benefits from Roosevelt's work during this decade.

The Young President

Theodore Roosevelt became vice president when President William McKinley began his second term on March 4, 1901. Six months later, an assassin shot McKinley. McKinley lingered a few days and then died. On that day, September 14, 1901, Theodore Roosevelt became the twenty-sixth president of the United States.

At forty-two, Roosevelt was young, enthusiastic, and eager to solve America's problems. He served the three remaining years of McKinley's term and won his own presidential election in 1904. During the first decade of the twentieth century, Roosevelt led America toward social reform, established a strong foreign policy, and began a conservation program.

Protecting the Environment

Roosevelt loved the outdoors. He liked to hike and hunt. He believed that all Americans for generations to come

The breathtaking scale and beauty of the Grand Canyon helped inspire Theodore Roosevelt to establish national parks.

should be able to enjoy the wilderness. He made this view clear in one of his speeches when he said that the Grand Canyon is "one of the great sights which every American . . . should see." He went on to tell Americans to leave it as it is "to keep it for your children, your children's children, and for all who come after you."[1]

As president, Roosevelt seized the opportunity to protect the beauty, natural resources, and wildlife in the western states. He established policies to protect special places in the United States such as Yellowstone, the Grand Canyon, and the redwood forest. He set aside 230 million acres of federal land that became the national forests, parks, and game preserves that people still enjoy today.

The establishment of the national parks remains one of Roosevelt's greatest accomplishments as president. Other presidents have followed Theodore Roosevelt's lead in protecting America's wilderness by increasing the federal land reserve and creating more national parks. Although protection of the wilderness was dear to Roosevelt's heart, he also cared about the well-being of the American people.

Roosevelt (center) poses next to a giant redwood tree. Roosevelt established parks to preserve special places like Yosemite.

Square Deal

Roosevelt thought that everyone in America should have the opportunity to prosper. He said, "If the average of well-being is high, it means that the average wage-worker, the average farmer, and the average business man are all alike well-off."[2] He called this a "Square Deal," and he wanted everyone, including farmers, military people, factory workers, miners, small businesspeople, and large companies, to have a square deal.

At this time, however, America was divided into groups including farmers, wage earners, and businesspeople. Each of these groups was interested in making life better for themselves. The farmers wanted higher prices for their produce. The wage earners wanted higher wages and better working conditions. The businesspeople wanted cheap labor and higher profits.

The result of all this was that as each group tried to help themselves, they hurt others. For example, companies expanded into big business with many departments. These departments performed services that the company would have bought from smaller companies. The small companies went out of business, and without competition, the large companies grew more powerful. No one could stop them from exploiting the workers.

The workers began to fight back. They wanted better working conditions and fair wages as a share of the companies' profits. They joined unions and went on **strike** to force the company to pay higher wages. Long strikes, however, hurt individuals and the nation. For example, the coal strike in the fall of 1902 not only threatened the company's profits, it meant no coal to heat homes and schools or to fuel other factories.

And farmers and food handlers, seeking higher profits, were sometimes careless in handling food. Sometimes they sold food that made the people sick.

A political cartoon of the era illustrates Roosevelt's dedication to improving the safety and quality of meat and other food products.

President Roosevelt believed that government should take steps to keep one group of people from hurting other groups of people and the nation. He also believed that "the welfare of each of us is dependent . . . upon the welfare of all of us."[3] As a result, he used his power as president to negotiate the end of the coal strike and better wages for the workers. He also used government to limit the size and power of large companies and rules for fair labor practices. And he established programs to assure the quality and safe handling of food from the farm to the grocery store. Many of these programs that Roosevelt established are the foundation for government programs that exist today.

Another area where Theodore Roosevelt established a foundation for today's policy was in world affairs.

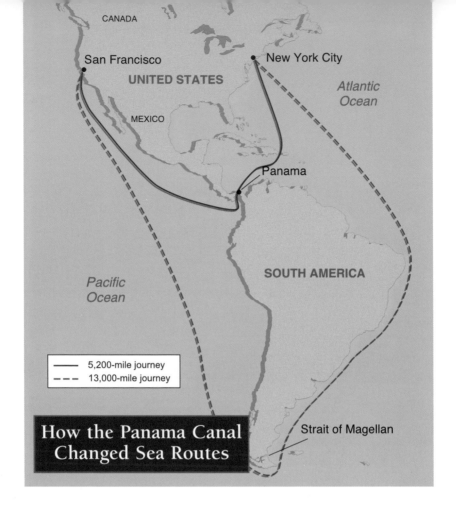

CANADA

San Francisco

UNITED STATES

New York City

Atlantic
Ocean

MEXICO

Panama

Pacific
Ocean

SOUTH AMERICA

—— 5,200-mile journey
– – – 13,000-mile journey

**How the Panama Canal
Changed Sea Routes**

Strait of Magellan

Panama Canal

In the first decade of the twentieth century, defending American shores was difficult because ships traveling from the East Coast to the West Coast had to go around South America's Cape Horn. A canal through Panama, however, would provide a shortcut through Central America and reduce the route from New York to San Francisco by almost eight thousand miles. Roosevelt believed that this would allow the U.S. Navy to better defend America as well as the whole Western Hemisphere.

In 1903, Roosevelt negotiated with Panama for the right to build and operate the Panama Canal. In the agreement, the United States also gained control of a five-mile strip of land on each side of the canal. This was known as the Canal Zone.

By this time, construction of the canal had already begun. In the late 1800s, a French construction company had tried to build the canal. Unfortunately, twenty thousand workers died of malaria and yellow fever, and the French abandoned the project after seven years. By the 1900s, mosquitoes were known to be carriers of these diseases. And American authorities knew to clear the area of standing water to prevent mosquitoes from breeding.

U.S. workers began work on the canal in 1904. Theodore Roosevelt visited the construction site in Panama in 1906. This was the first time a sitting American president traveled outside the United States. The canal was

During his presidency, Theodore Roosevelt protected the environment, created social reforms, and worked to maintain international peace.

Roosevelt sits in a steam shovel at the Panama Canal
construction site. The canal provided a shortcut for ships
sailing between the East Coast and West Coast.

completed in 1913, four years after Roosevelt left office. Still, the building of the canal resulted from Roosevelt's foresight and determination for a strong defense.

Nobel Peace Prize

Theodore Roosevelt's wisdom and leadership extended beyond the Western Hemisphere. In 1905, he negotiated a peace agreement between Russia and Japan, ending an international dispute without war. For this accomplishment, Roosevelt was awarded the Nobel Peace Prize in 1906.

The Roosevelt Era was a time of change as the nation experienced industrial growth and many people moved from rural areas to cities. Although many people worked long hours, they had more extra cash and leisure time than ever before. And people in small towns as well as big cities wanted entertainment.

CHAPTER TWO

Variety Theater

At the turn of the century, producers and managers of the **legitimate theater** (plays) in the large city theaters began to notice the need for entertainment in smaller cities and towns. With this in mind, they began booking acts to travel by train to small theaters across America. Soon, almost every town with a population large enough to provide an audience had a stage of some sort. As the demand for entertainment increased, chains of theaters were built across America. These theaters ranged from simple stages in barns to palaces with luxurious decor.

These traveling acts filled the **bill** for two forms of variety theater—vaudeville and burlesque. Vaudeville acts were clean family entertainment. Burlesque was **risqué**, with girlie shows and crude comedians that catered to working-class men. Vaudeville entertainers did not perform at burlesque theaters unless they had failed in vaudeville. Some burlesque acts, however, revised their routines and moved up to vaudeville.

Traveling Acts

Vaudeville acts included almost anything entertaining, such as trained animals, dance teams, comedy skits, one-act plays, comedians, singers, chorus lines, musicians, jugglers, acrobats,

Entertainment acts like the Imperial Burlesquers performed in traveling shows, entertaining the working-class across the country.

A vaudeville performer juggles hats during a skit. Vaudeville acts remained popular until the introduction of full-length motion pictures.

skaters, cyclists, magicians, orchestra, choirs, and big production numbers.

Each act brought its own set, costumes, and props. Large sets were usually assembled in a large eastern city. Many acts brought their own stagehands to handle all the tasks involved in preparing the set for the performance. A large production with a massive set and costumes for many dancers, singers, and musicians usually hired some local stagehands to help the traveling crew. These jobs provided temporary employment and helped the local economy.

Almost anyone with an act that pleased the crowd could get a job. On the other hand, any act that failed to please the crowd was canceled immediately. Canceled acts were often stranded far from home with no train ticket and no money. Still, show business was their life, and they loved the vaudeville stage.

Vaudeville

The word *vaudeville* came from an old French phrase, *Vau de Vire*. The phrase refers to the valley of the Vire River in Normandy, France, where composer Olivier Basselin lived in the fifteenth century. He wrote light, festive songs that became known as "songs of the Valley of Vire." Later this

Vaudeville shows usually had eight acts, and were performed in theaters like this one in Seattle, Washington.

became a song style and the word was shortened to *vau-de-vire*. Songs of this style became the basis for vaudeville entertainment and the source of its name. Vaudeville was very popular in the 1900s and continued as a major source of entertainment until it was replaced by full-length motion pictures.

A vaudeville show usually had eight acts, although some had as many as fourteen. The acts were presented one after another in a specific order. For example, an eight-act bill began with a quiet act that would not be ruined by noise as the audience arrived. This was often acrobats or animals. The second act was usually a song or dance team. They were usually billed as a sister or brother act. The third act was a comedy sketch or one-act play. Sometimes a Broadway star made an appearance here. A novelty or dance act usually took fourth billing, and a falling or rising star appeared before intermission. The second half opened with an act involving a large set with an animal act, choir, or novelty orchestra. The next-to-last spot was reserved for the star, usually a top vocalist or comedian that everyone wanted to see. And the last act was usually a boring or annoying act that encouraged people to leave the theater before the next show.

Variety Performers

Each show bill included a variety of acts to appeal to a wide range of entertainment tastes. Entertainment ranged from ordinary song-and-dance routines to outrageous shockers such as people who swallowed objects and brought them back up. In fact, Houdini, best known as an escape artist, swallowed needles and *appeared* to bring them up threaded on a string.

In 1906, as a stunt, Harry Houdini escaped from the jail cell that had held the convicted assassin of President

Garfield, Charles Guiteau, who was hanged in 1882. As a result, he gained national recognition as an escape artist and earned top billing on the vaudeville circuit. His escapes thrilled the audience with life-threatening dangers.

A young comic performs in a vaudeville act with his parents. Many entertainers of the era got their start in vaudeville.

For example, in one of his daring escapes he freed himself from padlocked chains while locked in a water-filled milk can.

A completely different type of entertainer, Will Rogers, earned a spot on the vaudeville stage as a "cowboy lasso expert"[4] in 1905. He roped a horse that his partner rode

Will Rogers (pictured), got his start in vaudeville. His humor and commentaries on American life brought him lasting fame.

around the stage. With each cast of the lasso, he roped a different part of the horse—sometimes the head, sometimes the front hoof, and so on. His roping skill fascinated the audience. Making humorous comments about his view of life and politics, however, brought him lasting fame. His homespun humor included such remarks as "Everything is funny as long as it is happening to Somebody Else."[5] In the years to come, Will Rogers became known as an American humorist. Many of his comments apply to life and politics today.

Most of the vaudeville stars are gone now. However, many entertainers that are remembered as radio, movie, and television stars learned their trade in vaudeville. In the 1900s, vaudeville offered a start in show business to promising entertainers and employment for stage workers. For almost everyone except the star, however, the hours were long, work was hard, and the pay was low. These people were members of the American workforce that grew rapidly in the 1900s, and laws were needed to protect them.

CHAPTER THREE

The American Worker

The dawning of the industrial age in the late 1800s brought new job opportunities to America. As industry expanded, a large number of workers was needed in factories that manufactured the growing number of new products. More workers were needed to build power plants that created electricity to light homes and operate the new electric appliances. Miners were needed to mine coal to power the electric plants and factories. Railroad and dock workers were needed to transport the factories' goods to market.

To fill this huge need, people began moving from farm communities to the cities. And more immigrants than ever came to America. As a result, America's cities experienced rapid growth. Industry and rapid urban growth created problems along with opportunity.

Immigration to the United States, 1900–1909

	1990–1909
Total in Millions	8.2
Percent of Total From:	
Ireland	4.2
Germany	4.0
United Kingdom	5.7
Scandinavia	5.9
Canada	1.5
Russia	18.3
Austria-Hungary	24.4
Italy	23.5

Source: David Ward, *Cities and Immigrants* (1971), p. 53.

An Italian family arrives at Ellis Island. America's cities expanded in the late 1800s as immigrants came in search of opportunity.

Working Conditions

As industry expanded and the demand for products increased, factories bought more steel and coal. Everything moved across the nation by railroad—steel, coal, and the manufactured goods. This increased business for the railroads. Times were good for almost everyone except the workers. In the rush to produce and transport the goods, employers had little concern for workers' safety.

The most dangerous industries were railroad and coal mining. In 1900, half of all worker deaths in the United States happened in these two industries. For example, coal miners spent long hours each day in dark, cold, damp,

Many immigrants found employment in construction. Here, laborers work in a railway tunnel.

Coal mining presented dangers to children who worked in the mines, and shortened many of their lives.

poorly ventilated tunnels. Many miners died from breathing poison gas. Others were crushed when tunnels collapsed. Those who were not killed by accident usually developed **black lung** from breathing coal dust.

At that time, industries took no responsibility for death or injury on the job. Companies did not pay medical costs or death benefits. Accidents were thought to be the workers' bad luck.

Child Labor

Bad as these working condition were for adults, they were worse for children. Sadly, many boys worked in the mines with their fathers. Boys who began work in the mines usually worked there the rest of their lives. Few miners lived past their early 40s.

Children worked at any job they were tall enough and strong enough to handle. No one worried about their safety, education, or health. Most working families needed the child laborer's income to put food on the table.

According to the 1900 census, about 1.75 million children between ten and fifteen years of age were working in the United States at that time. The census did not count

A girl rests after working all day in the Lancaster cotton mills. Most children worked to help feed the family.

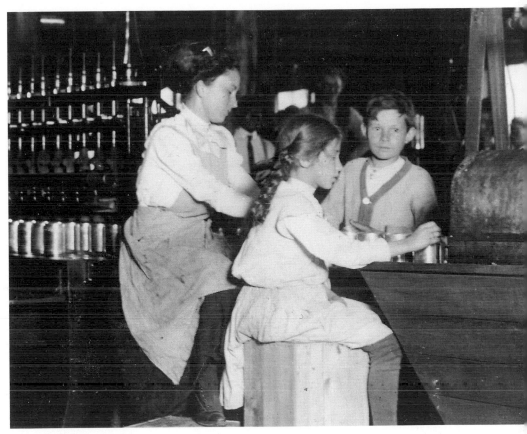

An eight-year-old girl works in a cannery. Child laborers worked long hours, were paid little, and rarely went to school.

younger children who worked in mills, factories, and on the streets selling newspapers and magazines. When these children are included, the number of child laborers rises above 2 million.

The young workers were paid very low wages. For example, a boy working in the Loray Mill in Gastonia, North Carolina, in 1908 was paid sixty cents a day for sweeping the floor. "When I sweeps double space I get 90 cents a day,"[6] he told photographer Lewis W. Hine. He probably worked twelve hours a day, six days a week. A girl working in the Lancaster Cotton Mills in South

Carolina was paid fifty cents an hour. A six-year-old berry farm worker in Maryland received two cents for each box of berries she picked. She usually picked two boxes of berries a day.

Some child laborers worked as much as seventeen hours a day. Many worked twelve to fifteen hours a day. They rarely received any formal education. Furman Owens started working in the mills in South Carolina when he was eight. When he was twelve, he did not know the alphabet and could not read. He said, "Yes I want to learn but can't when I work all the time."[7] With no education, these children had little hope of getting better jobs when they became adults.

Working long hours did not allow children to go to school and get an education.

Employers were not concerned about health hazards or safety for the young workers. Child laborers worked with sharp knives and suffered cuts and slashes. Others lost limbs in rotating machinery. Sometimes girls' long hair was caught in the machinery. In the worst case, the machinery pulled a portion of a girl's scalp from her head.

Many of the child laborers worked most of their waking hours. As a result, they had no chance to run and play. Lack of exercise along with poor nutrition caused stunted growth. Some of the tasks the children performed on the job changed the growth pattern of young hands, arms, and legs. As a result, many child laborers were damaged for life.

Making Changes

In an effort to stop child labor abuses, reformers created the National Child Labor Committee in 1904. They wanted to stop companies from using child labor. Powerful mine and mill owners fought this attempt. They did not want to lose the cheap labor. They ignored the fact that wages were too low and argued that families needed child labor to support themselves and that this hard work actually helped prepare children for adult life in industrial America.

The committee continued working for child labor reform throughout the decade. They gathered photos and statistics to present the plight of working children to the American people as well as Congress.

Lewis Hine was a dedicated reformer who committed himself to helping these children. He quit his teaching job in New York and began working for the National Child Labor Committee as a photographer. With his camera, Hine documented the abuses of child laborers in the 1900s. His work, however, was not completed until the

This child's back is bowed by the constant bending his job requires. In the early 1900s, two million children under the age of sixteen were employed in hazardous jobs like mining.

next decade. When the photos were published, America became aware of the child labor situation. People began to think about children and their role in the future of the nation. They realized that if children did not have opportunities to better themselves, the whole nation would be doomed to decline.

Labor Reforms

As a result of the committee's work, the **Children's Bureau** was founded in 1912. A year later, the Children's Bureau became part of the Department of Labor in the federal government. Finally in 1916, Congress passed the first federal legislation regulating child labor.

During this decade, other reformers worked to improve conditions for American workers. Labor unions such as the American Federation of Labor and the Industrial Workers of the World battled industry and business for better working conditions and higher wages. Over the years, they won the right for workers and companies to negotiate contracts that include better working conditions and better wages. Today, labor unions and business management continue the battle to balance workers' benefits and rights with management's needs and profits.

CHAPTER FOUR

The Automobile Age

The twentieth century and the automobile arrived in America about the same time. In 1900, the automobiles in America were used for racing. They were toys for the rich. The average working person could only dream of owning one. By 1905, however, vaudeville entertainers were singing a song about a young man taking his girl for a ride in his "merry Oldsmobile." By the end of the decade, the average worker's dream of owning a car was on its way to becoming reality.

Birth of the American Auto Industry

The American automotive industry was born in the 1890s when the Duryea brothers' American-built motor wagon raced against Europe's best models in the Chicago *Times-Herald* Race and won.

After the race, the Duryea brothers made plans to build motor vehicles to sell. Still, few motor vehicles would be produced for sale until the first decade of the twentieth century.

While the Duryea brothers were experimenting with their motor wagons, Ransom E. Olds was experimenting with steam, electric, and gasoline engines. Eventually, he chose a gasoline engine for his horseless carriage. Olds, however, was not thinking about racing his vehicles. He was thinking about building many vehicles to sell.

The Oldsmobile

Olds opened Detroit's first automobile factory. In 1901, the company produced 425 cars. The curved-dash Oldsmobile weighed 650 pounds and had an easy-to-remember price, $650.

Most people in America, however, were not ready to accept this new mode of transportation. They preferred the horse. And this new invention was noisy. It stirred up dust. It smelled. And it scared the horses. So, Mr. Olds had to convince people that the Oldsmobile was better than a horse.

Sheet music like these shown, and songs about automobiles, helped make automobile ownership popular by the end of the decade.

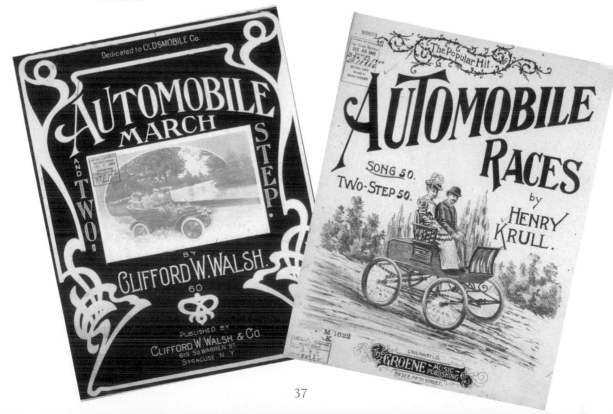

After experimenting with steam, electric, and gasoline engines, Ransom E. Olds chose a gasoline engine for his car, the Oldsmobile.

Olds thought of a plan to prove the value of his curved-dash runabout. He had Roy E. Chaplin drive the Oldsmobile from Detroit to Manhattan. The destination was the 1901 New York Auto Show. The road from Michigan to New York was a rutted wagon trail that tested Olds's workmanship. The sturdy Oldsmobile completed the trip in seven and a half days. It used thirty gallons of gasoline and averaged fourteen miles to the gallon. This successful journey made the Oldsmobile the talk of the auto show. As a result, Olds sold 425 Oldsmobiles in 1901. Business improved, and annual sales reached 5,000 in 1904.

Many people jumped into the automobile-building business. By 1908, there were 241 companies making automobiles in the United States. One of these was the Ford Motor Company.

Ford Motor Company

Henry Ford was one of the early automobile pioneers. He built his first automobile in 1896. Like the other automotive pioneers, Henry Ford raced his cars. When he decided to go into the auto business, his associates advised him

Automobile ownership allowed people to see more of the country and take longer trips.

to build large, expensive cars. In 1903, however, he opened the Ford Motor Company to build medium-priced cars for sale. These cars sold for one thousand to fifteen hundred dollars.

By 1905, the automobile industry was expanding, with about fifty new automobile manufacturers entering the business every year. There were not enough well-to-do customers to buy all the cars being produced. By 1908, many of these automobile companies were going out of business. Ford's business partners still thought the best way to improve business was to build fancy, expensive cars for the rich. Ford had a better idea.

The Model T Ford

According to Lee Iacocca, who began his career as a Ford employee, Henry Ford "figured that if he paid his factory workers a real living wage and produced more cars in less time for less money, everyone would buy them."[8] In other words, Ford wanted his employees to be able to afford the automobiles they produced. He began working on his idea in 1908 with the production of the Model T.

The first Model T sold for $850. It would be years before Ford actually produced the $360 Model T most people could afford. However, he worked on the problem several ways. Ford later said that "nothing is particularly hard if you divide it into small jobs."[9] He designed a sturdy car with no frills. He improved the **assembly line** and production methods. He opened dealerships across the country to sell the Model T. He encouraged people to open service stations to supply fuel for the cars. He worked to get reasonable traffic laws passed. And, most important of all, Ford improved working conditions and raised wages. In order to attract workers, other companies had to follow Ford's lead.

By improving working conditions and production methods, the Ford Motor Company produced affordable cars, like the Model T (pictured).

It took more than twenty years for Ford to realize his dream. Henry Ford is remembered for founding the Ford Motor Company. However, his greatest accomplishment was improving working conditions and raising wages, which turned America's workers into America's middle class.

The people, ideas, and leaders of the 1900s laid the foundation for the success of social programs that were developed throughout the twentieth century.

Notes

Chapter One: The Roosevelt Era

1. Theodore Roosevelt, Arizona, May 6, 1903. www.theodoreroosevelt.org.
2. Theodore Roosevelt, speech at the New York State Fair, Syracuse, New York, September 7, 1903. www.theodoreroosevelt.com.
3. Roosevelt, New York State Fair. www.theodoreroosevelt.com

Chapter Two: Variety Theater

4. Bryan B. Sterling, ed. *The Will Rogers Scrapbook*. New York: Grosset and Dunlap, 1976, p. 20.
5. Quoted in The Quotations Page, Will Rogers quotes. www.quotationspage.com.

Chapter Three: The American Worker

6. Quoted in Jim Zwick, "How Much Did Child Workers Earn?" The Campaign to End Child Labor. www.boondocksnet.com.
7. Quoted in Child Labor in America 1908–1912: "Photographs of Lewis W. Hine," The History Place. www.historyplace.com.

Chapter Four: The Automobile Age

8. Lee Iacocca, "Henry Ford," *Time 100*, April 1998. www.time.com.
9. Henry Ford. www.thinkexist.com.

Glossary

assembly line: A method of building a product in which each worker assembles a certain part of the product.

bill: The list of acts in a vaudeville or burlesque show, usually placed on the billboard outside a theater to advertise the show.

black lung: A serious lung disease caused by breathing coal dust.

Children's Bureau: The first government agency formed to protect children.

exploit: Taking unfair advantage.

legitimate theater: Plays performed in fancy theaters in large cities.

risqué: A little nasty or sexy.

strike: Workers refuse to work until the employer grants them better wages and/or better working conditions.

For Further Exploration

Judy Alter, *Vaudeville: The Birth of Show Business*. Danbury, CT: Franklin Watts, 1998. An easy-to-read, illustrated book about vaudeville performance and entertainment.

Jennifer Armstrong, *Dear Mr. President: Theodore Roosevelt Letters from a Young Coal Miner*. New York: Winslow Press, 2001. A historically correct fictional account of a young coal miner writing about his life to President Theodore Roosevelt.

Susan Campbell Bartoletti, *Growing Up in Coal Country*. New York: Houghton Mifflin, 1996. A factual account with black-and-white photos about child labor and the life of a young coal miner.

Michael Dooling, *The Great Horseless Carriage Race*. New York: Holiday House, 2002. An illustrated, easy-to-read account of the Chicago *Times-Herald* motor vehicle race in 1895.

David Fantle, *The Vaudeville Songbook: The Story, Stars, and Fifty Songs of Vaudeville*. Milwaukee: Hal Leonard, 1995. This book features profiles of popular vaudeville stars and includes words and music to fifty songs that made them famous.

David Weitzman, *Model T: How Henry Ford Built a Legend*. New York: Crown, 2002. This book tells the story of Henry Ford and his Model T and how he made the assembly line work better.

Index

automotive industry
  Henry Ford and, 39–41
  number of cars, 8
  origin of, 36
  Ransom Olds and, 36–38

Basselin, Olivier, 21
black lung, 29
burlesque, 18

cars. *See* automotive
  industry
census, 30–31
child labor, 29–33
Children's Bureau, 35
coal mining, 28–30
conservation, 9–11

Duryea brothers, 36

entertainment. *See*
  vaudeville

food handling, 12–13
Ford, Henry, 39–41
Ford Motor Company,
  39–41

Grand Canyon, 10

Hine, Lewis, 31, 33, 35
Houdini, Harry, 22–24
immigration, 26

invention, 6
  see also automotive
  industry

labor practices. *See* working
  conditions
Lancaster Cotton Mills, 31
life expectancy, 8
lifestyle, 6
Lorey Mill, 31

McKinley, William, 9
Model T Ford, 40

National Child Labor
  Committee, 33, 35
national parks, 9–11

Olds, Ransom E., 36–38
Oldsmobile, 37–38
Owens, Furman, 32

Panama Canal, 14–17
population, 8

roads, 8
Rogers, Will, 24–25
Roosevelt, Theodore
  awarded Nobel Peace
    Prize, 17
  conservation and, 9–11
  establishment of work
    programs by, 13

Panama Canal and, 14–17
terms as president, 9

safety
  child laborers and,
    29–33
  coal mining and, 28–29
  see also working
    conditions
Square Deal, 12
strike, 12, 13

unions, 12, 35

vaudeville
  description of, 18–22

performers, 22–25

wages
wilderness preservation,
  9–11
working conditions
  child labor, 29–33
  exploitation of workers,
    12–13, 28–33
  Ford Motor Company
    and, 40–41
  industrialization and, 6, 8,
    26–29
  labor reform and,
    33, 35
  wages, 8

Picture Credits

Cover Photo: © Bettmann/CORBIS
© Bettmann/CORBIS, 20, 27
© CORBIS, 7, 11, 28
Chris Jouan, 8
Collections of Henry Ford Museum and Greenfield
    Village, 41
Corel Corporation, 10
Fred Hultstrand History in Pictures Collection, NDIRS-
    NDSU, Fargo, 38
© Hulton|Archive/by Getty Images, 15, 16, 23, 24, 32
Library of Congress, 30, 31, 34, 37, 39
Library of Congress, Prints and Photographs Division, 19
Library of Congress, Prints and Photographs Division,
    Detroit Publishing Company Collection, 29
© North Wind Picture Archives, 12
© PEMCO-Webster & Stevens Collection, Museum of
    History & Industry, Seattle/CORBIS, 21

About the Author

Deanne Durrett is the author of nonfiction books for kids from third grade to high school. She writes on many subjects and finds research and learning exciting. She now lives in a retirement resort community in Arizona with her husband, Dan. Other members of the household include Einstein (a mini-schnauzer) and Willie (an Abyssinian). You can visit her website at www.deannedurrett.com.